Hedonism and eudemonism in Aquinas — not the same as happiness

TIMOTHY A. MITCHELL, Ph.D.

FRANCISCAN HERALD PRESS
1434 West 51st St. • Chicago, Ill. 60609

Hedonism and Eudemonism in Aquinas — not the same as Happiness, by Timothy A. Mitchell, Ph.D. Copyright ©1983 by Franciscan Herald Press, 1434 West 51st Street, Chicago, Illinois 60609. Made in the United States of America.

Library of Congress Cataloging in Publication Data:

Hedonism and eudemonism in Aquinas — not the same as happiness.

(Synthesis series)
Bibliography: p.
Includes index.
1. Thomas, Aquinas, Saint, 1225?-1274—Ethics. 2. Happiness—History. 3. Ethics, Medieval. I. Title. II. Series.
B765.T54M54 1983   171′.2′0924   83-20650
ISBN 0-8199-0926-2

Published with Ecclesiastical Permission.

October 21, 1983

MADE IN THE UNITED STATES OF AMERICA

CONTENTS

The Aim of the Synthesis Series 5

Introduction 9

CHAPTER 1
*Dewart's Notion of Spiritual
Hedonism in St. Thomas Aquinas* 13

CHAPTER 2
*An Examination of
Hedonism and Eudemonism* 21

CHAPTER 3
From Maritain to St. Thomas Aquinas 30

CHAPTER 4
*General Doctrine of
St. Thomas Aquinas on Happiness* 38

CHAPTER 5
*Specific Teachings of
St. Thomas Aquinas on Happiness* 51

CHAPTER 6
Conclusion 58

Bibliography 61

ACKNOWLEDGMENT

From proofreading to typing to offering suggestions and making corrections in a study like this one is indebted to many and so it is wise to mention none, else one is forgotten.

However, an exception must be made and mention given to Fr. John B. Mulgrew, now teaching philosophy at Molloy College in New York, who guided the thesis and unstintingly gave of his time to direct the author toward a proper understanding of the Angelic Doctor's teaching on the matter.

Dr. Timothy A. Mitchell

EDITORIAL PREFACE

THE AIM OF SYNTHESIS SERIES

As the growing edge of knowledge increases its pace and widens the domain of man, new vistas strike us which are both exciting and frightening. Although the spreading light reveals more and more the marvels of our universe, still the bordering darkness of the unknown expands along with it.

Nowhere is the uncharted field of the universe of being more deeply felt today than in the area which concerns man himself. Here especially our growing knowledge deepens awareness of the vast unknown beyond our present range of vision.

We have begun to realize that the project of comprehending man is indeed gigantic. It is the conviction of all who seriously contemplate the problem that only a multi-disciplinary approach and synthesis will produce a true picture. We find emerging a cooperative effort by those engaged in any discipline which bears upon understanding man and promoting his well-being. The human sciences, the arts, philosophy, religion and all the helping arts reveal him in the several dimensions of his complex pattern of life.

SYNTHESIS SERIES is intended to introduce the reader to the experience of using the multi-disciplinary approach when attempting to understand himself and others. We believe this will lead to his perceiving and relating to the entire human family more effectively — that is, more in accord with the rich depth and breadth of all those realities it contains. We hope this will help reduce the confusion caused by the over-simplified "answers" to problems of living which used to be offered by specialists in various fields.

Instead of the easy or quick answers, we propose that each individual make steady, serious efforts to achieve a rich synthesis of concepts developed by many disciplines. This appears to be the only method that holds the promise of yielding the fundamental answer — the meaning his own existence is supposed to have — a meaning so often fretfully and falteringly sought by everyone whether he admits it or not. The promise and its realization in personal experience provide sufficient motive to undertake and sustain the search. But beyond this, one can foresee benefits which transcend individual well-being. For personal growth of many individuals brings about a **social atmosphere** which stimulates still further development toward a more meaningful life on the part of each member of the group.

This interaction between an individual and others is apparent when we observe the opposite process of deterioration. Just as the most disruptive factor in society is the unrest caused by failure of its members to find the meaning of life, so the reverse holds true, that society will benefit at all levels in proportion to the success people have in their quest for the meaning they believe their existence is supposed to have.

SYNTHESIS SERIES, we repeat, is intended to introduce the reader to the new multidisciplinary method in carrying out the search for the meaning his life is to have when viewed in reference to the destiny of mankind.

INTRODUCTION

The question of hedonism in the systematic thought of a saint and mystic, St. Thomas Aquinas, whose whole life was devoted to God, is — to say the least — paradoxical. Moreover, the paradox has been deepened with the addition of an adjective, "spiritual," so that "spiritual hedonism" has sometimes been attributed to St. Thomas Aquinas. Although the phrase was formulated by Leslie Dewart and is uniquely his,[1] it would be a mistake to think that the notion is his alone.[2]

Since its coinage, the term has raised occasional discussion in the quarterlies and monthlies, but despite the great array of Thomistic scholars, some of whose writings we shall examine, there has not been (as far as we can determine) any outcry against its usage. Indeed, scholarly comments have sometimes been advanced in its favor.

Fr. Verhaar, S.J., in his answer to Michael Novak's critical review of Dewart's *Future of Belief*,[3] attempted to defend the formulation by saying that Dewart revealed "two dualisms to be traced back to the hellenic mind . . . between the knower and the known; and . . . between pessimism and the urge for happiness. The former can be traced in the history of philosophy as much to Kant as to Marx, the latter to Freud."[4] The important point, Verhaar stressed, is that

Dewart "criticizes Thomism (old and new) mainly on the ground that it has perpetuated (this) hellenic frame of reference."[5]

Dewart shows, he continues, that in the perspective of faith, "a concern for truth can be and often is confused with an obsession for clarity; and further that the urge for happiness may tend to love the gift rather than the giver."[6] Thus Fr. Verhaar comes to the heart of Dewart's thought; but the distinction in St. Thomas that separates Thomas from both the hedonistic philosophers and the eudemonism of Aristotle is never mentioned. We are left, instead, with a distinct feeling that the judgment of spiritual hedonism has been seconded.

In casting a resounding *no* against this verdict, we shall begin by analyzing the pertinent passages from *The Future of Belief* and allowing Dewart, as it were, adequate time to state his case. By so doing, two things will be accomplished: the thesis that St. Thomas was a spiritual hedonist will be fully aired, and our critique will have a structure from which to build.

Next, we shall clarify the meanings of the three basic terms which Dewart homogenized into one: "hedonism," "eudemonism," and the "beatitude" of St. Thomas Aquinas. After we review the history and philosophy of hedonism, and contrast it with eudemonism, we shall show that, even though both are egocentric in nature, they are not — as Aristotle also taught — synonymous.

Then we shall turn to the beatitude of St.

Thomas, looking first at the "basis" of Dewart's position, namely, the writings of Jacques Maritain, and, juxtaposing them alongside part of the Thomistic corpus, we shall point out that both the idea that Aquinas was a hedonist and that Maritain sees him as such are erroneous interpretations.

Having stated the objection, that St. Thomas was *not* a hedonist, we shall move to the heart of the argument by scrutinizing the pertinent passages of the Angelic Doctor and, with the help of some commentators, shall establish that because of its objective orientation, the Thomistic notion of happiness is radically different from both hedonism and eudemonism.

This study of the writings of St. Thomas Aquinas will comprise our last two chapters. Chapter 4 will examine his general doctrine and concentrate on two aspects of his thought: his insistence that the beatitude of man is objectively, rather than subjectively, oriented, and his definition of divine friendship. Chapter 5 will concentrate on two questions in the *Summa Theologiae*: whether man's happiness consists in pleasure and whether happiness, like pleasure, consists in some good of the soul.

NOTES

1. Leslie Dewart, *The Future of Belief* (New York: Herder and Herder, 1966), pp. 28–35, 74.
2. Walter Kaufman, in his *The Faith of a Heretic,*

attributes the same teaching to Christianity, noting that Trolestch perpetrated the same idea. Fr. De Lavallette tells us that the same path was trod a half-century ago by Laberthinmere, whose criticisms were leveled "against the hedonism of Thomistic morality." See Gregory Baum, *The Future of Belief Debate* (New York: Herder and Herder, 1967), pp. 37–42.

3. Michael Novak, "Belief and Mr. Dewart," *Commonweal*, Feb. 3, 1962, pp. 485–488.

4. Fr. John W. M. Verhaar, S.J., "Dewart and the New Neo-Thomism," *Continuum*, 5, no. 4 (1968), 635.

5. Ibid. This is, of course, the central theme of the work, but it is an area where Frederick Wilhelmsen (*Triumph*, Jan. 1967, pp. 30–34) claims that Dewart is not radical enough, for he fails to understand that with Thomas' progression from Avicenna, the dehellenization of Christianity was done years ago. And this is why, he continues, Gilson never stops repeating that the revolution of St. Thomas in metaphysics was so radical that it even escaped his immediate disciples. Fr. Lonergan has criticized Dewart on the same point. In an article in *Theological Studies* (June 1967, pp. 336–351), he attacked the notion that Greek philosophy supplied the basic concepts for the formulation of the Incarnation and the Trinity. He refers to the authoritative study of G. Prestige (*God in Patristic Thought*, pp. 197 and 209) on the use of the word "homoousics" as a metaphor drawn from natural objects and not of Greek origin.

6. Ibid.

Chapter 1
DEWART'S NOTION OF SPIRITUAL HEDONISM IN ST. THOMAS AQUINAS

In his *Future of Belief,* Dewart tells us that, for "St. Thomas, the fulfillment of man's perfection, that for the sake of which he exists, is happiness, since 'happiness means (for Thomas) the acquisition of the last end.' To be sure, [this] fulfillment consists in a spiritual and indeed supernatural happiness, . . . But (since the object of man's happiness is God) this refers to happiness considered in relation to its object as such."[1] In the last analysis, then, St. Thomas' ethical doctrine — according to Dewart — "rests on the hellenic principle that man's perfection is happiness."[2] This is so, he concludes, because "St. Thomas based his doctrine of morality on the Aristotelian idea that human purposiveness and striving are intelligible only in terms of a final cause."[3]

In attributing this premise to Thomas, Dewart has done two things: he has laid the groundwork for his own philosophy of "ethics for the future" and he has structured the foundation of his understanding of the ethical doctrine of St. Thomas. It is on this second aspect that we shall concentrate, since the first aspect has been adequately stated by Dewart himself.[4]

Dewart begins his quasi-Thomistic ethical structure by imputing a spiritually hedonistic position to Maritain and then identifying Maritain's thought with that of St. Thomas, and then transfers the imputed position to Thomas. "No less unexceptionable a Catholic thinker than Jacques Maritain," Dewart says, "has, though hardly in so many words, admitted that the Christian morality of beatitude (that is, happiness) can take the illusionary form[5] described by Freud."[6]

In support of this contention, Dewart unknowingly undercuts his argument by presenting Maritain's position in the latter's *Moral Philosophy*: Although "theologians are perfectly clear on all this, . . . that is that Christian morality is a morality of beatitude, . . . nevertheless first and foremost, it is a morality of the divine Good supremely lived."[7] For Maritain is simply repeating the thought in the Act of Contrition: "I detest all my sins, because I dread the loss of Heaven and the pains of Hell, but most of all, because they offend Thee, my God, who art all good and deserving of all my love." The issue should now be resolved in Dewart's disfavor — but no, he goes boldly on.

Nevertheless, Dewart reminds us, Maritain "has written 'popular preaching' [Dewart's frame of reference has momentarily shifted] is often inclined to put the emphasis above all, if not even exclusively, on the joys of the reward and the pains of punishment."[8] Dewart grants the differences between "the theologian" and "popular preaching,"[9] but concludes that even though popular preaching is an oversimplified version of what theology (and the magisterium) teach, "it is not a corruption or contradiction of it."[10] The frame of reference has again shifted to "the theologians," and Dewart moves in for the kill.

By continuing his thought with the following, Maritain, he insists, seeks to justify the practice of the popular preacher:

These [the joys of reward and the pains of punishment] are truths which immediately stir our natural fear of suffering. And even if one insists *only* on them, one can always *hope* that once the sinner is turned toward the subsistent Good from motives of which love of self hold first place, the living faith will thereafter make him spontaneously subordinate his own interest to God loved first.
After all, one lends only to the rich. And the preachers of the Gospel feel themselves excused in advance, if, in the arguments by which they push in toward salvation, they employ *without too much scruple* a kind of eudemonism, even hedonism, *at least ambiguous in character,* in the service of the love of God.[11]

Dewart, having convinced himself of the "hedonism" of Maritain, now examines its "development" in St. Thomas Aquinas. This long tradition, of which Maritain is not solely typical,[12] he argues, goes back to early (if not primitive) Christian times and is reflected in both the Scholastics and the magisterium.[13] For Thomas, it is grounded in the Grecian principle that the perfection of man is happiness. Is there, then, a

15

difference between this principle and the classical doctrine of hedonism? Yes, answers Dewart,[14] for according to St. Thomas, "that 'happiness [which] is man's supreme perfection . . . must consist in man's last act.' "[15]

Dewart then refers us to the Thomistic distinction between "happiness" and "delight"; but claims that their concomitance "logically implies that the attainment of delight [of the right sort, to be sure] can provide a practical criterion for the moral conduct of life."[16] Therefore, even though it might not be "Christianly perfect," there is nothing basically wrong "with seeking ultimate delight for its own sake," because it "is natural for man to seek happiness with all his might."[17] For who but the mystics and saints can truly know what it is to love God more than themselves.[18]

Man's perfection, then, consists in happiness; and "though he may not know its source, it remains true that to desire happiness is nothing else than to desire that one's will be satisfied."[19] Thus, hedonism, according to Dewart, is the ground of the ethical doctrine of St. Thomas.

However, Dewart is quick to remind us, this doctrine is not without qualifications. There is much in St. Thomas, he goes on (by way of clarification), that qualifies this hedonism,[20] but nothing (as far as he can see) that "retracts the position" or is of a "theoretically more basic nature."[21] The last point is emphasized, because of the moral certainty — the man, after all, is a saint, that Thomas "did not practice what he preached" — another "proof" for Dewart that the Scholastic synthesis of faith and reason "was less than perfect." And precisely because of this less-than-perfect synthesis, Maritain was able to blame "the preachers," rather than "the theologians," for spreading spiritual hedonism.[22]

That the preachers have exaggerated the idea is tentatively granted by Dewart, but only after he tells us that it might be more truthful to proclaim that the "eudemonism" of the preachers is the result of the "spiritual hedonism of Scholasticism."[23] We must admit its existence, and without shame, for "under certain historical and cultural conditions this was the logical way . . . in which the truth of Christianity could be cast." "No one need be ashamed if when he was a child, he spoke as a child."[24]

This, then is the argument — a line of reasoning that not only fails to distinguish between hedonism and eudemonism, but unqualifiedly identifies both of them with the "happiness" of St. Thomas Aquinas. As such, it overlooks the crucial distinction between the objective attainment of the good and the connective but subjective satisfaction that necessarily accompanies such possession. Consequently, it completely misses the thrust of the Thomistic doctrine.

Happiness, for St. Thomas, as Dewart correctly notes, is man's ultimate end — but it is not the hedonistic striving for egoistical pleasure. Rather, it is the desire to please the one who is loved.

Out of love God made man, that man might

be happy with God in heaven. Man, following the same impulse, responds to that love by doing precisely what all lovers do: obeying the wishes of the loved one. In other words, man seeks heaven not because it will make him happy (which it necessarily will do), but because God, whom he loves, desires it.

Because Dewart maintains his position by identifying the happiness of St. Thomas with both hedonism and eudemonism, it is necessary to review the meanings of these three terms. In the next chapter, then, we shall present a brief history of hedonism, followed by an examination of its philosophical premises. Next, we shall turn to a study of eudemonism and discover that, while there is a difference between the two philosophies, they resemble each other in that both are oriented toward subjective satisfaction. In the following chapters, we shall subject the philosophy of St. Thomas to a searching analysis, studying his writings and those of the noted commentators.

NOTES

1. Dewart, *The Future of Belief,* p. 30.
2. Ibid., p. 32.
3. Ibid., p. 30.
4. This principle, we are told in a footnote on p. 32, "would convey the idea that the moral self-fulfillment of man is intrinsically connected with his ontological self-realization rather than with his affective reaction to

reality as an object set off from him. The ontological perfection of man, his free and self-creative coming-into-being, overflows into moral perfection because man does his existing in the presence of God. What man makes himself to be, therefore, places him in a certain existential situation in relation to God. Man's purposiveness and striving, thus, reside in his seeking creatively, not to be happy, but to be. The Christian doctrine of grace can be totally integrated with this idea, if we keep in mind that the free self-creation of man takes place in the presence of God not only insofar as it constitutes man's final achievement, but also insofar as it constitutes his constant present being" (ibid., p. 32).

5. For Freud, an illusion (and here he is concerned with the "illusion" of religion) is not an error. An illusion is a belief which has wish fulfillment as a prominent factor in its motivation, and which disregards its relation to reality (*Future of an Illusion,* pp. 53–55). Dewart, as we shall see, does not chide Maritain or the Church for their "illusions," but merely wants them to grow out of "childhood."

6. Op. cit., p. 28.
7. Jacques Maritain, *Moral Philosophy* (New York, Scribner, 1964), p. 79.
8. Op. cit., p. 28.
9. Ibid.
10. Ibid., p. 29.
11. Ibid.
12. Dewart also finds spiritual hedonism in *Moral Values and the Moral Life* by Etienne Gilson. From p. 19 of that book he quotes the following to make his point: "Morals is the science of how man is to conduct himself so that the story of his life may have a happy ending" (*The Future of Belief,* p. 28).
13. Op. cit., p. 29.
14. See footnote 2.
15. Op. cit., pp. 30–31.
16. Ibid., p. 31.
17. Ibid.
18. Ibid., p. 32.
19. Ibid.
20. Dewart admits here that Thomas explicitly and implicitly teaches that perfection does not consist only

in this attainment of happiness through the gaining of an objective end. Whenever he taught this, he presented "a view which was truly Christian, but which could not be reconciled with [his] hellenic approach to ethics" (p. 33).

21. Op. cit., p. 33.
22. Ibid.
23. Ibid., pp. 33, 34.
24. Ibid., p. 35.

Chapter 2
AN EXAMINATION OF HEDONISM AND EUDEMONISM

Hedonism

Fr. Buckley, in his study of man's last end, came to the heart of our question when he observed that the threefold division of Aristotle is characteristic of the history of philosophy.[1] This division, he noted, comprises the three most typical aspects of life: the contemplative, the political, and the pleasurable.[2] Thus the ends are reason, duty, and pleasure.

Pleasure, Buckley wrote, has been sponsored as a "last" end since the days of Aristippus. However, he quickly added, not all who have held this position have looked upon pleasure as *man's* last end; because they reject objective values, "their moral criterion is certain in the final analysis to be subjective feeling."[3] Thus hedonism, whether it is man's final end or not, is defined as a rejection of objective values for subjective feeling.

Almost all philosophers, Buckley notes, have distinguished among various forms of pleasure, insisting upon the superiority of the spiritual. But "even spiritual enjoyment, when it is sought for its own sake rather than for the object whose value justifies our joy, is empty and vain."[4]

Hence, Buckley concludes, no matter how much the superiority of the spiritual is stressed, "their followers have gone the logical incline . . . to the position of the absorption in sensuous pleasure, popularly attributed to hedonism."[5] Thus, in Buckley's view, all hedonism, even hedonism of a spiritual nature, is subjective and devoid of objective content — a position which, we shall show, pervades the history of the philosophy of disciples of pleasure.

Hedonism, as a philosophical system, finds its roots in the "conduct theory" of Aristippus of Cyrene (435-356 B.C.).[6] For him, "the basis for practical conduct" is individual sensations and its end is "to obtain pleasurable sensations."[7] He proclaimed that sensation is fleeting and "consist[s] in motion."[8] Gentle motion is pleasurable whereas rough motion causes pain, but since motion cannot be an ethical end, the ethical "must, therefore, be pleasure, a positive end."[9] Thus pleasurable sensations are the end of life — but are they bodily or intellectual pleasures? Fr. Copleston, S.J., tells us the bodily pleasures were regarded as more "intense and powerful" and, therefore, preferred.[10]

Later, Hegesias was so convinced of life's miseries that the emphasis shifted from a positive to a negative concept.[11] The *absence* of pain was stressed. For Epicurus, the goal was *ataraxia,* a state of mind resulting in "tranquil happiness, free from pain, fear, and unrest."[12] For Hegesias, the end was absence of sorrow and pain, with cool indifference to gratifying acts.[13] Anniceris, on the other hand, stressed the positive; he sought gratification in individual acts, but limited this to acts of friendship and gratitude and love of country and family.[14]

The above is only a sketch of classic hedonism, yet it encompasses the main point that concerns us here: hedonism for the Greeks, in its final form, was primarily subjective.[15] Until the seventeenth century, its praxis as a philosophical system was "more or less dormant," even though "there were many who embraced its practical excesses."[16] Then, after Bishop Joseph Butler's devastating refutation, exposing its egoistic tendencies,[17] the center shifted to universalism: the greatest happiness for the greatest number (best represented by Bentham and Mill).[18] Because universalism concerns the many and not the one, it has no direct bearing on the individualistic hedonism of which St. Thomas is charged by Dewart, but it regards pleasure in the same subjective way as individualistic hedonists and it contains the same philosophical positions.

These two positions, according to R. L. Cunningham, are ethical hedonism and philosophical hedonism. The first makes pleasure the only good that *should* be desired while the second posits that nothing but pleasure *can* be desired. But the two positions conflict, because, strictly speaking, the latter view cannot be reconciled with the former. "If we can desire nothing but pleasure, it is surely pointless to recommend pleasure, as the only thing that ought to be desired. . . . Nevertheless, history reveals that some men have

23

held both positions, such as Epicurus and Bentham."[19]

To sum up: The hedonist claims that "absolutely pleasant experiences are intrinsically valuable; and further, that only pleasures are intrinsically valuable; and further, that what is 'morally good' is identical with, or instrumental to, pleasant experience."[20]

Therefore hedonism, like most errors, is an exaggeration of one aspect of the truth, to the exclusion of the other aspects. And, like most errors, it goes astray not in what is affirmed but in what is denied. Because the good is considered only in its relation to pleasure, it "tends to cynical egoism, founded on identification of men with God, forgetting that God is, and man is not, the supreme good."[21] Thus it affirms pleasure in terms of a homocentric supreme good and aims, in the words of Fr. Garrigou-Lagrange, "at happiness but excludes obligation."[22]

Now that we have seen that the ultimate end of hedonism is subjective, we shall look at the eudemonism of Aristotle to see if, as Dewart holds, it is synonymous with hedonism.

Eudemonism

In the *Nichomachean Ethics* (I, 1097 B1), Aristotle sharply distinguished hedonism from eudemonism when he wrote that we "always choose eudemonism on its own account, and never with an eye to something further; whereas honor, pleasure, mind, and every excellence we choose on their own account, it is true . . . but we choose them also with an eye to eudemonia, conceiving that through them we shall be in possession of eudemonia."[23]

Stephen Rueve, taking note of this distinction, wrote that "Aristotle considered happiness and pleasure . . . two entirely different things, as shown by passages too numerous to be quoted."[24] He also pointed out that, in the tenth book of the *Nichomachean Ethics,* happiness is "a serious operation,"[25] not "an amusement which is pleasant."[26] The same can be more clearly seen when we view Aristotle's discussion of friendship.

Friendship, as taught in the tenth book of the *Nichomachean Ethics,* makes "it plain that pleasure is not the good or else there are different classes of pleasure."[27] For friends associate with us "with a view to the good" while the flatterer is our companion "with a view to pleasure." The latter is reproved while the former are praised.[28] The conclusion drawn by Aristotle from this example is that pleasure does not constitute the good, nor should every pleasure be pursued.[29]

After discussing the things that have to do with pleasure and friendship, Aristotle, turning to the question of eudemonism, said it "would be absurd if the end were amusement and if trouble and hardship throughout life should be all for the sake of amusing oneself."[30] Except for eudemonism, "which is itself the end, everything we choose is for the sake of something else." Even a slave "might enjoy the pleasures of the body. But no one allows a slave a share in happiness, anymore than in political life. Happiness does not consists of such things, but of activities in accordance with virtue."[31]

Thus, for Aristotle, eudemonism is not pleasure; but it must be noted that it is not completely divorced from pleasure, for the Philosopher clearly stated that he thought " it essential that pleasure should be mixed in with happiness."[32] And for this reason primarily, hedonism has been attributed to Aristotle.

Concluding his article on pleasure and happiness in Aristotle, Dr. Rueve called attention to the fact that many writers view Aristotle as a hedonist. However, Aristotle steadfastly refused this classification, both in "the sense of considering pleasure the norm of morality" and in "the sense of considering pleasure as man's summum bonum."[33] Thus the twin pillars on which a hedonistic philosophy is structured were rejected by Aristotle.

The same conclusion was reached by William Callaghan in his outline of the philosophy of Aristotle, in which Callaghan lists several arguments against the notion.[34] To begin, he observed, the Cyrenaics and others, while they differed on the definition of pleasure, contended that all pleasures are good by the simple fact of their pleasureableness. But, Aristotle answered, many of these would-be pleasures are not pleasures at all.

Secondly, unlike the hedonists, who claimed that all pleasures are good, Aristotle insisted that all pleasures are not good. Rather, they share the same moral character as the activities from which they proceed. Thus some are good and some are not.

Finally, and most importantly, Aristotle departed sharply from hedonists who held that pleasure is the ultimate goal in life. It is not, for the primary positive pleasures accompany activities which we would do whether they are pleasurable or not, simply because we are made to act in such a manner. In the main, we are creatures who talk, reason, eat, and move about; and of lesser import, when all is right, pleasure is derived from these activities.

Thus we see that the terms "eudemonism" and "hedonism" are not synonymous, though Dewart contends that they are, and they should not be used interchangeably. Rather, in Aristotle's view, they are to be distinguished in that the former constitutes the ultimate end while the latter is an activity that leads to the ultimate end.

It remains for us, therefore, to determine whether the happiness of St. Thomas Aquinas is in any way synonymous with either of these two different views or as Dewart implies, with both. But because Dewart used the philosophy of Maritain to substantiate his position, it is necessary that we begin our analysis of the happiness of St. Thomas by examining the writings of this modern philosopher. Then, by juxtaposing them alongside part of the Thomistic corpus, we shall show that the notion that St. Thomas was a hedonist, and that Maritain viewed him as such, is wrong on both accounts.

NOTES

1. Fr. J. Buckley, *Man's Last End* (se. Louis: Herder and Herder, 1949), p. 49.
2. Ibid., p. 8.
3. Ibid., p. 11.
4. Ibid.
5. Ibid.
6. Brother Charles Reutemann, F.S.C., *The Thomistic Concept of Pleasure,* Abstract Series, vol. 5 (Washington, D.C.: Catholic University Press, 1953), p. 25.
7. Fr. Frederick Copleston, S.J., *A History of Philosophy* (New York: Image Books, 1950), 1, pt. 1: 107.
8. Emile Brehier's *History of Philosophy,* Vol. II: *The Hellenistic and Roman Age* (Chicago: University of Chicago Press, 1965), pp. 18–19. The notion that pleasure consists in motion was demolished by Plato in the *Philebus.*
9. Op. cit., p. 142. See also Diogenes Laertius, *Lives of the Philosophers* (*Third Century*), 2, 86ff.
10. Ibid., Copleston, p. 143.
11. Ibid., pp. 143–144.
12. Op. cit., Reutemann, p. 25.
13. Op. cit., Copleston, p. 143.
14. Ibid., vol. I, pt. I, p. 144; vol. I, pt. II, p. 154.
15. Brehier seems to bring an exception to the rule. Eudoxus of Cnidas, he tells us, was known for his "austerity and reserve" and yet was a hedonist, "not on account of his taste for pleasure, but rather to bear witness to truth" (*The Hellenistic and Roman Age,* pp. 18–19).
16. Op. cit., Reutemann, p. 25.
17. Bishop Joseph Butler, *Fifteen Sermons,* ed. W. E. Gladstone, in *Complete Works of Butler* (London: Oxford Press, 1897).
18. James Mill was a disciple of Bentham.
19. R. L. Cunningham, "Hedonism," in *New Catholic Encyclopedia,* 6: 983.
20. Ibid., p. 984.
21. Fr. Reginald Garrigou-Lagrange, *Beatitude* (St. Louis: Herder and Herder, 1937), p. 20.
22. Ibid., p. 23.

23. Stephen J. Rueve, "Aristotle on Pleasure and Happiness," *Modern Schoolman* (May 1936), p. 82.
24. Ibid., p. 83.
25. *Nichomachean Ethics* X 1177 a 2.
26. Ibid., X 1176 B9.
27. *The Philosophy of Aristotle,* tr. A. E. Wordman and J. L. Creed (New York: Mentor Books, 1963), pp. 363–364.
28. Ibid., p. 364.
29. Ibid.
30. Ibid., p. 369.
31. Ibid.
32. Ibid., pp. 369–370.
33. Rueve, op. cit., p. 83.
34. William J. Callaghan, *An Outline of the Philosophy of Aristotle* (Boston: Student Outline Co., 1959), p. 50.

Chapter 3
FROM MARITAIN TO ST. THOMAS AQUINAS

Happiness and Pleasure in the Philosophy of Jacques Maritain

In the voluminous writings of Jacques Maritain, one can easily point to many passages that indicate that the ultimate end of man in the philosophy of St. Thomas is theocentric and oriented toward happiness, and is not, as Dewart claims, hedonistically egocentric. Throughout his life, Maritain tenaciously maintained this position, and perhaps its clearest exposition is in his *Introduction to Philosophy,* where he wrote:

The fundamental question which practical philosophy must answer before any other is in what consists (from the standpoint of the natural order) the last end or absolute good of man. . . . On the fundamental question of ethics — the question of man's last end — we find for the last time the schools of philosophy divided roughly into three groups. The school of Aristotle and St. Thomas teaches that the entire moral life depends on man's tendency to his sovereign good or happiness and the object in which the happiness consists is God — whom, moreover, we ought to love, not for our own sake, but for Himself (precisely because He is our last end, that is to say, that which is willed and loved for itself, not for the sake of anything beyond) . . .

for the greatness of man consists in the fact that his sole end is the uncreated good.[1]

Thus Maritain, by drawing a distinction between the objective and subjective end and pointing out that, for St. Thomas, man's ultimate goal is objectively oriented, separated him from hedonism, which, as we have just demonstrated, is primarily directed toward subjective attainment. It now remains to be seen whether the same separation can be made between St. Thomas and eudemonism.

In his discussion of the Kantian ethic, Maritain sharply distinguished between eudemonism and the happiness of St. Thomas when he observed: "Kant cut the moral life off at the same time from Aristotelian Happiness and from Christian Beatitude, [that is] from all impetus toward a supreme transcendent felicity."[2] Then, as if in anticipation of Dewart, Maritain attributed the precise notion of spiritual hedonism to Kant and, by positing what he called the "subjective ultimate end," rejected the notion as part of the Thomistic system.

Neither "the natural aspiration toward happiness . . . nor the aspiration to partake of the divine beatitude, which for [Thomas] derived only from a kind of transcendent eudemonism or even hedonism, was involved in the proper order of morality."[3] For "the subjective ultimate end, which in the original perspective of revealed ethics was the superfulfillment of the being and the desires of the human subject through the vision of God, and the joy which derives from it as an inherent property, are definitely banished" by St. Thomas "from the order of morality."[4]

In conclusion, Maritain noted that by "rejecting the desire for happiness from the proper order of morality, Kant renounced the possibility of making it transcend itself, and of freeing it from eudemonism."[5]

Having rejected the idea that eudemonism and the happiness of St. Thomas are synonymous, Maritain, in discussing the absolute ultimate end, came to the heart of Dewart's position. It is very difficult, he wrote, still analyzing Kant, "for a rationalist philosophy to understand that a being which naturally desires happiness can love another being, even God, otherwise than for its own selfish sake."[6] In a Kantian way of thinking, whatever the mystics say, to "act for the love of God" would still be "to act out of that love of self which . . . is the reason for all other love."[7] "In the last analysis, it would still amount to seeking one's own happiness in a concealed way, to obeying an interested motivation, to fall off from pure disinterestedness."[8]

Probing the analysis further, Maritain showed that, with an ethical theory built on an ontological foundation which takes account of both lines of causality, the final and the formal, it is possible to understand that a moral act can depend upon both lines simultaneously. It "derives its intrinsic value from its conformity to its formal rule, and it is accomplished in virtue of a motivation which derives from finality."[9] Thus, in the traditional sense, "a good man does that which is good (or in conformity with reason, the formal rule) for love of subsistent Good (final causality)."[10] On the other hand, one can understand that a subordination of ends is possible. A good act may be motivated by personal interest or love of self but be subordinated "to a supreme motivation," namely, the love of God.[11] This hierarchy of ends, then, precludes the identification of hedonism and Thomistic happiness in the thought of Maritain.

To put the association beyond plausibility, Maritain summed up his study of the absolute ultimate end in Kant — rather, the lack of it — with these words:

The disinterestedness which following the very channels of our natural desire for happiness, but catching that desire in the trap of love as it were, begins by subordinating to the love of the ultimate End, loved more than ourselves, the search for a supreme happiness that we still desire for love of ourselves (although primarily for the love of God). This disinterestedness comes to fruition in such a complete love of the absolute ultimate End, loved more than ourselves, that we no longer wish supreme happiness to ourselves except for love of that End, so complete a love that we even forget (without being able to renounce it) the search for the supreme happiness we wish for ourselves without having to think about it, since we only wish it for ourselves for the love of God, not of ourselves. Because genuine Christianity does not despise the natural desire for happiness and does not reject it from the proper domain of morality but directs it to something better and more loved, genuine Christianity transcends all eudemonism.[12]

Clearly, then, in Maritain's view, St. Thomas was neither a hedonist nor an eudemonist. So now we go directly to the writings of the saint.

Happiness and Pleasure in the Philosophy of St. Thomas Aquinas

Throughout his writings, as the following responses indicate, St. Thomas sharply distinguished between pleasure and happiness.

In replying to the question whether happiness is an activity of the intellect or the will,[13] he noted that, essentially, "it is impossible for it to be an act of the will. . . . For happiness is the attainment of the ultimate end." The will, however, which is directed to the end, both as absent "when it desires it" and as present "when it delights in resting in it, cannot of itself attain the end." And "delight is in the will as a result of the end being present." Therefore, St. Thomas concluded, "it must be something other than an act of the will by which the end becomes present to the one willing it."

Consequently, "the essence of happiness consisted in an act of the intellect, but the delight resulting from happiness belonged to the will." Thus happiness is distinguished from pleasure in that happiness is an act of the intellect while pleasure (or delight) is an act of the will.

Before he made this distinction, however, St. Thomas repeated the two things that are required for happiness[14] and further clarified, as it were, these differences. "One refers to the very being of happiness," he wrote, "and the other is a per-se accident of it, namely, the delight connected with it."

Again, St. Thomas noted that to "be the reward of virtue is accidental to beatitude or happiness, arising from the fact that some one attains to it; even as to be the term of generation belongs accidently to a being so far as it passes from potentiality to act."[15]

In the *Summa contra Gentiles,* this distinction between happiness and pleasure in the order of sense is clearly indicated. Pleasure is an operation of the senses but happiness is a capacity infinitely beyond the sensual. Pleasure can be sought instinctively by animals, but animals cannot be happy; so it is a mistake to attribute the capacity of happiness to animals.[16]

Pursuing the distinction in the order of sense, St. Thomas came to the same conclusion when he considered whether vision or delight is primary in happiness. "The Philosopher," he wrote, "says in the same passage[17] that 'delight complements activity as the bloom of youth, which is a result of youth, complements youth.' Consequently, delight is a certain perfection accompanying vision, not a perfection making vision perfect as to the kind of thing it is."[18]

Continuing the thought, Thomas came to the heart of the issue. So decisive was his response that it must be quoted in full:

The apprehending by sense does not attain the

universal notion of good but some particular good which is delectable. Hence animals seek activities corresponding to their sense appetites for the sake of the delight involved. But the intellect apprehends the universal notion of good, and the attainment of this results in delight. Hence it intends the good principally rather than the delight. This is the reason the divine intellect, which is the author of nature, joined delight to activities on account of the activities. But our estimate of things should be made not simply in terms of the order of sense desire, but rather in terms of the intellectual desire.[19]

With this important point established, namely, that both Maritain and St. Thomas distinguished between pleasure and happiness, we shall take a closer look at some of the writings by and about the Angelic Doctor in an effort to probe the distinction.

NOTES

1. Jacques Maritain, *An Introduction to Philosophy,* tr. E. I. Watkin (New York: Sheed and Ward, 1934), p. 267. The same theocentric thought is pithily stressed in *Science and Wisdom* on p. 163: "For our last end it would assign God efficaciously loved above all things by natural love."
2. *Christianity and Philosophy* (New York: Scribner, 1964), p. 100.
3. Ibid.
4. Ibid.
5. Ibid., p. 101.
6. Ibid.

7. Ibid.
8. Ibid.
9. Ibid., p. 104.
10. Ibid., p. 109.
11. Ibid., p. 104.
12. Ibid., p. 106.
13. *Summa Theologiae,* I–II, Quest. 3, art. 4.
14. Ibid., Quest. 2, art. 6.
15. Ibid., I, Quest. 26, art. 1.
16. *Summa contra Gentiles,* book III, ch. 27: *"Non enim bruta possunt dici felicia nisi abusive."*
17. *Nichomachean Ethics* X, 4 (1174B23).
18. *Summa Theologiae,* I–II, Quest. 4, art. 2.
19. Ibid.

Chapter 4
GENERAL DOCTRINE OF ST. THOMAS AQUINAS ON HAPPINESS

Two major aspects of St. Thomas militate against the notion that his doctrine of happiness was hedonistic: his insistence that man's beatitude is objectively oriented rather than subjectively, and his definition of the meaning of divine friendship. In this chapter, then, we shall examine these two topics.

Happiness is Objective, not Subjective

In the *Summa contra Gentiles,* St. Thomas agreed with Aristotle that, subjectively, man's final beatitude is eudemonistic, in a sense, and that it consists in speculation of the highest truths.[1] But it is here that they part company, and the "main difference between them," Fr. O'Connor wrote, "arises from the fact that Aristotle has no certainty of personal immortality, so that he necessarily locates man's ultimate happiness and end in the present life."[2] Thus, for St. Thomas, the ultimate end in Aristotle is contemplation and, as such, is regarded "from the subjective view alone."[3]

Along these lines, O'Connor observes, the end of man is a continual progression in happiness and wisdom, with the intellect never reaching the terminus of its activity. St. Thomas saw this as proper "in its own order,"[4] but it is not ultimate happiness, for he was well aware "that natural beatitude is not perfect beatitude, because it is essentially incomplete."[5] In the *Summa contra Gentiles* he came to the heart of this incompleteness:

And this seems to have been Aristotle's view on felicity. Hence in Ethics I, where he asks whether misfortunes take away happiness, having shown that felicity consists in the works of virtue which seem to be most enduring in this life, he concludes that these men for whom such perfection in this life is possible are happy as men as if they had not attained felicity absolutely, but merely in human fashion.[6]

The same thought was expressed in his *Summa Theologiae*:

Because Aristotle saw that man had no other knowledge in life beyond the speculative sciences, he concluded that man does not attain perfect happiness, but only in a human way.[7]

Again, in the *Summa Theologiae,* in answer to the question Does happiness consist in scientific knowledge? he dismissed "the beatitude of Aristotle as 'imperfect.' "[8] "Aristotle is speaking in the Ethics of imperfect happiness such as can be had in this life."[9]

Fr. O'Mahony noticed the same judgment of imperfect beatitude imputed to Aristotle by St. Thomas in article 4, ad. 4, of the same question[10] and attributed this to the metaphysical level of the saint's reasoning.[11] Because of his interest "in the metaphysical exigencies of beatitude, St. Thomas insists on the fundamental distinction of beatitude as objective and subjective. It can scarcely be said that Aristotle rose to a concept of beatitude that gave to the objective its priority over the subjective state."[12] In fact, O'Mahony concludes, the stress and orientation are in the other direction toward hedonism.

Aristotle's "silence on the question of the priority of pleasure or of vital activity," he argues, "seems calculated and . . . his treatise on *Friendship* seems to fall back into the merest hedonism."[13] Thus Aristotle's "insistence on the necessity of a final end has not the full significance that such a statement has on the lips of St. Thomas."[14]

The full significance of the final end led St. Thomas to exclude from the order of ultimate happiness any trace of its subjective tendencies. "Beatitude, as regards its object, is the highest good absolutely; but as regards its act, in beatified creatures, it is not the supreme good absolutely, but in the genus of goods in which a creature can participate."[15] For man "is not to be loved for his own sake, but whatever is in man is to be loved for the sake of God."[16]

Therefore, while St. Thomas was too much of an Aristotelian to disregard or, rather, "deny that everything seeks after its own good, and that therefore man, too does the same, he did not stop there," but developed "the thought until the individualistic or egoistic poison in the doctrine [was] all drained away."[17]

Thus, for St. Thomas, ultimate beatitude is measured objectively, rather than subjectively. The thought was brought out clearly as he answered the question, Can one be happy in this life?

Participation in happiness can be imperfect in two ways. One is on the part of the object itself of happiness, which is not seen according to its essence, and such imperfection does detract from the nature of true happiness. The other way is on the part of the one participating, who indeed attains the object of happiness in itself, namely, God, but imperfectly in comparison to the way God enjoys Himself. Such imperfection does not detract from the true nature of happiness because, since happiness is a certain activity as we have said,[18] the true nature of happiness is taken from the object which specifies the act, and not from the subject.[19]

Now that we have seen that St. Thomas not only considered eudemonism imperfect, but that his distinction between objective and subjective happiness separated him from both Aristotle and the hedonists, we shall look at his teaching on divine friendship, where the distinction becomes even sharper.

The Meaning of Divine Friendship

St. Thomas, following Aristotle, distinguished between real friendship as objective love (love for the person) and apparent friendship as sub-

41

jective love (love of oneself).[20] Now real friendship, Robert Sheehan tells us, "may be defined as a mutual well-wishing between persons who communicate," but "the motive must be for the real, not merely apparent, good of the person."[21] The thought was summed up by St. Thomas when he concluded that it is "evident that charity is friendship of man for God,"[22] which he drew deductively from a precise line of reasoning.

"It must be said," he began, referring to Aristotle,[23] that "not all love is friendship, but only the love of benevolence, when, to wit, we love someone so as to wish good to him. If, however, we do not desire good for him we love, but desire his good for ourselves . . . ,[24] it is love not of friendship, but of a kind of concupiscence."[25] Thus we see that, for St. Thomas, love of God for self is not charity but concupiscence.

Aristotle, when he discussed this question — in the view of one commentator, Fr. Jerome Wilms — not only excluded from the realm of friendship those who wished well "to the friend for the sake of utility or of pleasure arising to self; but [limited it] to the good who resemble each other in virtue."[26] St. Thomas, however, while following Aristotle in excluding self-seekers from the realm of friendship, deepened the thought with the addition of sanctifying grace and moved far beyond him and the hedonists. St. Thomas wrote:

Sanctifying grace in man is the effect of the divine love. Now the proper effects of the divine love would seem to be that man in return love God, since God's chief intention in loving men is that He be loved by men in return. Every lover seeks eagerly to meet with a response of love on the part of his beloved and, unless he succeeds, love must be broken off. Now men arrive at love of God by the inpouring of sanctifying grace into the soul.[27]

With this infusion of grace, Wilms writes, "man is morally obligated to conform himself to the divine will and desire and return love for love."[28] Thus we see that friendship for God is not merely the willingness to love a friend, but a moral obligation to do so. For charity, St. Thomas explicitly informs us, "touches God himself that it may rest in him, not to receive anything whatever from him."[29] This is so because "God directs righteous men to Himself as to a special end, which they seek, and to which they wish to cling; according to Psalm LXXII, 28, it is good for me to adhere to God."[30] Therefore, in the order of charity, man's desire for God, far from being a self-centered pursuit of pleasure, is obedience of the highest sort.

Fr. Wilms honed the thought to a fine edge and, by purifying it of egoistical tendencies, further separated it from the hedonism of either the modern or ancient type and from the eudemonism of Aristotle. He noted that wherever St. Thomas says "God as the final end is the object of love," he means that divine friendship to "which God, out of pure goodness, has called me, and for the acquisition of which he has fitted out my soul with certain capacities and rights — this same all-embracing divine goodness which is mine, that it is which I also wish him; and I am happy to know that it constitutes his perfection and his happiness."[31] He concluded a paragraph later: "Thus I rejoice that God, who is love itself and who with this very love loves me, is eternally happy in the goodness he exercises towards me."[32] Thus man loves God out of obligation and friendship.

St. Thomas, in a most precise manner, defined the meaning of this friendship. It is marked, he tells us, by the regard of a good simply as good.[33] He distinguishes it from concupiscence or self-love, where the good is sought for the pleasure of possession. Friendship, rather, seeks to give and, instead of possessing objects, permits them to possess him.[34]

The difference between the two loves was tersely presented by Fr. Wilms: "It is obvious that the act of charity differs from concupiscible love which desires all things for itself, even God, himself. This is purely crass egotism It is true that its odiousness may be temporarily veiled, if its immediate object is noble. But this state can never last permanently. Once recognized, such self-seeking is detested."[35] For St. Thomas, then, man's love for God is not the subjective pursuit of pleasure, but a desire for God in compliance with God's wishes.

"This love of desire which aims at possession," however, is "a love of God identical with love of self. For to love God thus is to love oneself in accordance with the highest exigencies of the natural impulsion; . . . it is to love oneself as one whom God, Himself, would make happy in the joy of this possession."[36] Therefore when "man loves himself in God and for God" and seeks to enjoy God and his glory, his act is an act of charity.[37] And this "movement of the human spirit towards the fruition of the divine Good is the proper act of charity whereby all the acts of the other virtues are ordered to this end."[38] Thus we see that, in the aspect of desire, charity bears a likeness to the love of concupiscence in "its eagerness, its open arms, its outstretched hands eager to take all that is good both in the order of nature and of grace."[39] But the *likeness* is not to be confused with *identification*.

Jean Mouroux's superb analysis of this teaching anticipates, as it were, the nature of "spiritual hedonism."[40] He observes that only a "fundamental misunderstanding could induce us to consider such a love (charity) as interested and egoistic." Egoistic love is a "deviation from the natural tendency" that results from sin, while charity, on the other hand, "is there precisely to restore, purify and divinize the natural tendency."[41] His conclusion is that "the act of desire that springs from charity, itself, cannot be egoistic, it is necessarily as right and true as the impulse whence it proceeds."[42]

He explains why this human desire is not egoistical. It is a love, he notes, that is bounded by "strict metaphysical conditions" and by "one who is not his own end," and whose end cannot be reached except "in possession and fruition of the Sovereign Good."[43] Such a love is "the sign of our condition, . . . and is necessarily pure and true." But this is not the highest love, "for love is more gift than desire."[44]

Love as gift (or friendship) shifts the center from man to God and the termination is no longer possession but communion.[45] It is now a giving rather than a receiving. God, now, "is a greater good than any other, . . . because He is more intimately present to the soul than is the soul to itself."[46] This is why Mouroux says that "the soul abandons itself to give itself over to God."[47] Charity, then, is a combination of love as gift (friendship) and love as desire, so that the love that has primacy will determine which love, to use Dewart's phrase, "is more basic in nature."

St. Thomas informs us that, by virtue of a general law, all love as desire is contained within love as gift, which clearly has primacy.[48] Thus love of "oneself as a real being . . . is something simply necessary, and this the love of desire . . . but to love oneself . . . as a person called, is something that goes deeper, something more radical and absolutely first, and this is the love of gift which goes to God while nevertheless enveloping the desire."[49]

Thus we see that love of charity has two aspects: one of desire and one of friendship. St. Thomas addressed the heart of the issue when he answered the question, Is love fitly divided into love of friendship and love of desire? Love tends "to the good which one wishes for a person," he wrote, and "to the person for whom one wishes the good." Therefore,

> towards the good . . . one wishes for some one the love of desire is entertained, but toward the person for whom one wishes that good, there is entertained the love of friendship. What is loved with a love of friendship is loved absolutely and by itself; but what is loved with a love of desire is not loved absolutely and by itself, but is loved for another. The love wherewith an object is loved that good may accrue to it, is love absolutely; but the love wherewith a thing is loved that it may be the good of another is love in a restricted sense.[50]

In the preceding two chapters we have made distinctions among the three terms and have shown that "hedonism," "eudemonism," and the "happiness" of St. Thomas Aquinas are not synonymous and should not be used interchangeably. We began with a brief sketch of hedonism to make the point that pleasure is subjectively oriented and egocentric. Next, we looked at the eudemonism of Aristotle and saw that, in the Philosopher's view, it differs sharply from pleasure; unlike pleasure, it is not sought for something else but is itself the ultimate end. As such, even though it is subjectively oriented, it lacks the total subjective stress of hedonism. Finally, we examined the happiness of St. Thomas and learned that, because of its total concentration on the object, there is no room for the egocentric poison that contaminates the other two positions. We indicated that because St. Thomas was so aware that natural beatitude is incomplete and thus imperfect, he soon parted company with Aristotle and insisted on a sharp distinction of beatitude as objective and subjective. For Thomas, man is neither to be loved nor to seek salvation primarily for his own sake (his salvation is sought for himself, but this, too, is for the sake of God), but whatever is in him is to be loved for the sake of God. His desire for God, then, is not just a desire for his own salvation, but a love for God and a wish — with the help of sanctifying grace — to do the beloved's will. And because of the infusion of grace, man's friendship for God is escalated beyond that of the creature to his ultimate end, to the level of divine friendship, so that there is a twofold moral obligation: to love God as ultimate end and to love him as supreme friend. Man, then, because of this twofold obligation, is drawn to God and rejoices in him. But this love of God is identical with love of self, as ordered to God, for to love God as such is to love oneself as the one whom God, in the joy of possession, would make happy. Thus all that is willed is sought not for self, but for God. Therefore the love of self is simply necessary, while the love of God is something deeper, more radical, unrestricted, and absolutely primary.

Now, having developed in a general manner these distinctions between pleasure and happiness, we shall concentrate on the two questions in St. Thomas which specifically bear upon the subject: Whether the happiness of man consists in pleasure and whether happiness, like pleasure, consists in some good of the soul.

NOTES

1. St. Thomas Aquinas, *Summa contra Gentiles* (Garden City, N.Y.: Image Books, 1955), book III, chs. 26–50.
2. Fr. William O'Connor, *The Eternal Quest* (New York: Longmans, Green, 1947), p. 198.
3. Ibid., p. 199.
4. Ibid.
5. Ibid., p. 200.
6. *Summa contra Gentiles*, book III, pt. I, ch. 48, art. 9.
7. *Summa Theologiae*, I, Quest. 2, art. 1, ad. 1.
8. Ibid., I-II, Quest. 3, art. 6, ad. 1, and art. 4, ad. 4.
9. Ibid., art. 6, ad. 1.
10. Fr. James O'Mahony, *The Desire of God* (Dublin: Cork University Press, 1929), p. 205.
11. Ibid., p. 203.
12. Ibid., p. 204.
13. Ibid.
14. Ibid.
15. *Summa Theologiae*, I, Quest. 26, art. 3.
16. Ibid., I–II, Quest. 2, art. 7.
17. Fr. Martin D'Arcy, *The Mind and Heart of Love* (New York: Meridan Books, 1956), p. 102.
18. *Summa Theologiae*, I–II, Quest. 3, art. 2.
19. Ibid., Quest. 5, art. 3, ad. 2.
20. *Nichomachean Ethics* IX 9 1169B.
21. Robert J. Sheehan, *The Philosophy of Happiness according to St. Thomas Aquinas* (an abstract) (Washington: Catholic University Press, 1956), pp. 4, 11.
22. *Summa Theologiae*, II–II, Quest. 23, art. 1.
23. *Nichomachean Ethics* VIII 2, 3.
24. St. Thomas lists as examples of this a glass of wine and a horse.

25. Two fine works on the nature of this love are Jerome Wilms' *Divine Friendship* (Dubuque: Priory Press, 1958) and R. Egenter's *Divine Friendship* (Minneapolis: Augsberg, 1928).
26. Wilms, *Divine Friendship,* p. 27.
27. *Summa contra Gentiles,* book III, ch. 151.
28. Op. cit., p. 34.
29. *Summa Theologiae,* II–II, Quest. 23, art. 6.
30. Jean Mouroux, *The Meaning of Man* (Garden City, N.Y.: Image, 1961), p. 231.
31. Op. cit., p. 39.
32. Ibid., pp. 39–40.
33. *Summa Theologiae,* I, Quest. 20, art. 1, ad. 3.
34. Ibid., I–II, Quest. 26, art. 4.
35. Op. cit., p. 42.
36. Mouroux, *The Meaning of Man,* p. 233.
37. St. Thomas affirms this on numerous occasions. See, for example, *Summa Theologiae,* II–II, Quest. 26, art. 13.
38. *Summa Theologiae,* I–II, Quest. 114, art. 4c.
39. Wilms, *Divine Friendship,* p. 46.
40. Thus the question was answered fifteen years before it was raised.
41. Op. cit., p. 233.
42. Ibid., pp. 233–234.
43. Fr. Wilms wrote of the love of desire as a love "which wants the good, even the highest — for itself, but self is united to, not separated from God." Because it belongs "no longer to self but to God, all that is willed and desired is willed and desired rather for God, . . . than for self." Such an act, he concludes, only "seems to be self-seeking but is not so in truth." It belongs, rather, "to the realm of charity" (*Divine Friendship,* p. 43).
44. Ibid., p. 234.
45. Ibid.
46. III *Sentences D.* 29, Quest. I, art. 3, sed. c. 2.
47. Op. cit., p. 235.
48. *Divinis Nominibus* IV, Lect. 9–10.
49. Mouroux, *The Meaning of Man,* p. 236.
50. *Summa Theologiae,* I–II, Quest. 26, art. 4.

Chapter 5
SPECIFIC TEACHINGS OF ST. THOMAS AQUINAS ON HAPPINESS

Does Man's Happiness Consist in Pleasure?

In the sixth article of the second question in Book I–II of the *Summa Theologiae,* St. Thomas came to the heart of the problem when he answered the above question. His response to the first objection — that since desire for pleasure as an ultimate end belongs more to happiness than anything else, happiness must consist most of all in pleasure — involves a sharp distinction between a formal cause and a final cause.

"We desire good," he began, "for the same reason we desire delight,[1] which is simply the resting of the appetite in a good." After demonstrating the point by comparing it to a heavy body that is borne downward to its resting place, St. Thomas concluded that delight, like the good, is sought for itself — if "for" is the proper word to denote a final cause. "Hence, just as good is sought for itself, so also is delight sought for itself and not for anything else, if 'for' expresses a final cause." But, he continued, if "for" denotes "a formal cause, or more the moving cause, delight is desirable for something else — for the good — which is the object of delight and, consequently, its principle and gives it its form; for delight is derived because it is resting in the desired good."

Thus his reply to the first objection distinguished between "end" in the order of final causality and "end" in the order of formal causality. Therefore pleasure is the end when, like the good, it is an expression of final cause, namely, a resting of the appetite in the good. But when the formal cause — that is, the cause that moves the will — is expressed by "for," pleasure is not the end but is sought for something else, namely, the good which is its object.

Disposing of the second objection with little difficulty, St. Thomas returned to the theme in the third question and reemphasized the point beyond doubt. The third objection postulated the following syllogism. The major premise stated that since "desire is of the good, it seems that all desire what is best." The minor premise added that all — the wise, the foolish, and even irrational creatures — "desire the delight of pleasure." Therefore the conclusion: "Such delight is better than all goods. Accordingly happiness, which is the highest good, consists in pleasure."

St. Thomas answered that all "desire delight in the same way as they desire good; yet they desire delight by reason of the good and not conversely, as said in the first reply." Thus delight is sought for the sake of the good; the good is not sought for the sake of delight. His conclusion was that "it does not follow that delight is a maximum and per-se good, but that every delight results from some good." The delight is not of itself an ultimate good; rather, it is either the result of, or follows upon, some ultimate good. This conclusion, that every delight is a result of some good, was reaffirmed in the response.

Because of the greater knowledge of bodily delights, the response began, the word "pleasure" has been given to them,[2] although other delights excel them. However, "happiness does not consist in them [because] there is a distinction between what pertains to the essence of a thing and its proper accident; thus, in man, to be a mortal rational animal is other than to be risible." St. Thomas then moved to the heart of the discussion when he noted "that delight is a proper accident which follows upon happiness or some part of happiness, for a man is delighted when he possesses some good suitable to him, either in fact or in hope, or at least in memory. Now a suitable good, if it is the perfect good, is precisely man's happiness; and if imperfect it is a certain participation in happiness, either proximate or remote, or, at least, seemingly so. Clearly, then, even the delight which follows upon the perfect good is not the essence of happiness, but something from it as a proper accident."

Thus pleasure, we see, is not the essence of happiness but, rather, something that accidentally follows upon attainment of its object of happiness. However, in terms of perfection, pleasure is required for happiness.

In response to the three objections that pleasure

(or delight) is not a requirement of happiness, St. Thomas wrote:

One thing may be required for another in four ways. First, as a preliminary and a preparation for it, and thus teaching is necessary for science. Second, as perfecting it, and thus the soul is necessary for life of the body. Third, as an extrinsic aid, and thus friends are needed for some undertakings. Fourth, as something concomitant, and thus we might say that heat is needed for fire. It is in the last way that delight is required for happiness. For it is caused by desire being at rest in the good attained, and since happiness is the attainment of the highest good, it cannot be without a concomitant delight.[3]

Now that it has been shown that, in the Thomistic system, happiness does not consist in pleasure — even though pleasure is a concomitant requirement for perfection — we shall direct our attention to the next perplexing question: Whether happiness consists in some good of the soul.

Does Happiness Consist in Some Good of the Soul?

Article 7 of this question was approached through an examination of three articles.[4] The first runs as follows: Since happiness is a human good and a human good consists of external goods — goods of the body and goods of the soul — happiness must be one of these. But since it has been shown that the first two alternatives have been eliminated,[5] it follows that happiness "consists in goods of the soul."

The second moves syllogistically in two stages. It begins by positing that we love that for which some good is desired more than we love the good that is desired for it.[6] And since everyone desires all goods for himself, it follows that everyone "loves himself more than all other goods." Now, since it is evident — from the fact that all other goods are desired for its sake — that happiness is that which is loved above all, happiness must consist "in a good of man himself." But, as we noted above, since this is not a good of the body, it follows that it must be a good of the soul.

And the third states that since "happiness is a perfection of man" and perfection or "fulfillment is something belonging to that which is fulfilled . . . happiness is something belonging to man." And again, since this "is not something of the body," it can only be "something pertaining to the soul" and, thus, "consists in goods of the soul."

But St. Thomas answered no in the *sed contra,* for St. Augustine tells us that "which constitutes a life of happiness is to be loved for itself."[7] However, he continued, drawing upon the wisdom of these words, man "is not to be loved for his own sake, but whatever is in man is to be loved for the sake of God. Therefore, happiness does not consist in any good of the soul." Thus in two sentences Thomas answered the three arguments that purport to make happiness a good of the soul, on the ground that it is sought for the sake of man.

But Thomas honed the thought to perfection, and his response began with a reassertion of the definition.[8] End, St. Thomas reminds us, is spoken of in two ways: "of the thing itself which we desire to obtain, and of the use, attainment, or possession of that thing."[9] Now if we are talking about man's ultimate end, "it is impossible," St. Thomas wrote, "that the ultimate end of man be the soul or something pertaining to the soul. For the soul, considered in itself, is like a being in potency, for it becomes knowing in act from knowing in potency, and virtuous in act from virtuous in potency. But since potency is for the sake of act, as its fulfillment, it is impossible that what is in itself a being which is in potency have the nature of an ultimate end. Hence, it is impossible that the soul be its own ultimate end."

The second conclusion St. Thomas reached in this response is that nothing that belongs to the soul — be it a power, a habit, or act — can be man's ultimate end. Thus happiness does not consist in any act of the soul, as it does in a beatifying object. And since delectation or pleasure is an act of the soul, it can be concluded that happiness does not consist in pleasure.

However, in the third conclusion in this section Thomas explained that if the ultimate end is spoken of as possession, attainment, or the use of an object desired as an end, "then something of the part of the soul of men does pertain to the ultimate end, since man attains happiness through the soul." Therefore the thing itself — that is, the objective end — "is that in which happiness consists and makes men happy, but the [subjective] attainment of that thing is called happiness." Thus, it must be said "happiness is something belonging to the soul, but . . . the object of happiness is something outside the soul."

The point is that happiness does not consist in some good of the soul, and since pleasure is a good of the soul, it follows that happiness does not consist in pleasure.

NOTES

1. John Oesterle tells us that the Latin word which is used in this article is *delectato*. It means "delight," "satisfaction," or sometimes "gratification." "A certain sort of delight," he goes on, "is what St. Thomas usually means by 'delectato,' though like 'pleasure,' it may belong either to intellect or sense. The latter is primarily intended here" (*Treatise on Happiness* [Englewood Cliffs, N. J.: Prentice-Hall, 1964], p. 22 quotation).

2. St. Thomas refers us to the *Nichomachean Ethics*, VII, 13.

3. *Summa Theologiae*, I–II, Quest. 4, art. 1.

4. Since these three arguments fairly well cover the spectrum of egocentric happiness, it is well that we present them in some detail, for in countering them, St. Thomas neatly undercuts the groundwork of Dewart's contention.

5. *Summa Theologiae*, I–II, Quest. II, art. 1–5.

6. St. Thomas gives the example of loving a friend "for whom we desire money more than we love the money."

7. St. Augustine, *On Christian Doctrine*, I, 22.

8. The definition was asserted in Quest. I, art. 8, of the *Summa Theologiae*, I–II.

9. Here St. Thomas is truly Aristotelian, for the principle is drawn directly from the *Physics*, II, 2 (194A35).

Chapter 6
CONCLUSION

In this brief study we have tried to demonstrate that the term "spiritual hedonism," as used by Leslie Dewart to define the doctrine of St. Thomas, has no basis in fact.

We began by explaining that even though the formulation is Dewart's special product, the notion is not his alone, nor was he the first to use it.

To present the question adequately, we opened with a careful analysis of the pertinent passages from Dewart's *Future of Belief*. Consequently, the full implications of the interpretation became manifest at the outset and the direction of our critique took on form.

Our first task in attempting to get to the roots of St. Thomas was examination of the two principal terms, which Dewart had blended into a whole. We compared "hedonism" and "eudemonism" and showed, after reviewing the history and philosophy of the former and the philosophy of the latter, that, while both are egocentric, they cannot — as Aristotle also insisted — be used interchangeably.

Next, following Dewart's lead, which sought to make his thesis credible by appealing to and claiming Jacques Maritain as a proponent of the same idea, we looked at two of Maritain's writings and contrasted them with some of the Angelic Doctor's. Our conclusion is that not only is there no basis for asserting that Maritain taught — or believed St. Thomas taught — that man's desire for beatitude is a venture in spiritual hedonism, but that Maritain's writings and those of St. Thomas clearly indicate the opposite.

After pointing out the proper direction of Thomistic thought on beatitude and Maritain's correct understanding of it, we directed our attention more fully to the writings of St. Thomas Aquinas and began, in effect, the heart of our study, which completely severs Thomas from any hedonistic-eudemonistic affiliation.

We indicated that St. Thomas was so aware that the "natural happiness" of Aristotle is incomplete that he completely parted company with him and insisted upon the sharp distinction of "objective" and "subjective happiness." For Thomas, man is not to be loved or even to seek salvation, primarily for his own sake, but — whatever is in him — is to be loved primarily for the sake of God. And since God has ordered man to Himself as ultimate end, man rejoices when out of obligation he is drawn to God. In a word, man seeks God as a friend not for pleasure, but from a desire to please the Loved One, which necessarily brings him pleasure.

Having established this distinction, we substantiated it by analyzing two basic questions: Whether happiness and pleasure are the same, and whether happiness is the good of the soul. Allowing the saint to do his own talking, we showed that happiness and pleasure are not one and that happiness is not a good of the soul and, ergo, is not pleasure.

This, then, concludes our study of the notion of "spiritual hedonism." If it has clarified the question, it will make us very happy; but in true Thomistic fashion, it was not the ultimate end of its inception.

BIBLIOGRAPHY

I. Primary Sources

Aquinas, St. Thomas. *Commentary on Ethics* (VIII–IX). Tr. Pierre Conway. Providence, R. I.: Providence College Press, 1951.

———. *Summa contra Gentiles.* Tr. Charles J. O'Neill, Anton Pegis, James Anderson, and Vernon Bourke. 5 vols. Garden City, N. Y.: Image Books, 1955.

———. *The Pocket Aquinas.* Ed. Vernon Bourke. New York: Washington Square Press, 1960.

———. *The Teacher, the Mind, Truth.* Questions X, XI. Tr. James V. McGlynn, S.J. Chicago: Henry Regnery Co., 1953.

———. *The Trinity and Unicity of the Intellect.* Tr. Sister Rose Emanuella. St. Louis: Herder Book Co., 1946.

———. *Treatise on Happiness.* Tr. John A. Osterle. Englewood Cliffs, N. J.: Prentice-Hall, 1964.

Pegis, Anton C., ed. *Basic Writings of St. Thomas Aquinas.* New York: Random House, 1948.

Dewart, Leslie. *The Future of Belief.* New York: Herder and Herder, 1966.

II. Secondary Sources

Adler, Mortimer J. and Walter Farrell, O.P. "The Theory of Democracy," pt. III. *The Thomist,* vol. 4.

Baker, Richard R. *The Thomistic Theory of the Passions.* South Bend, Ind.: Notre Dame Press, 1960.

Bastable, P. K. *Desire for God*. London: Burns, Oates and Washbourne, 1947.

Baum, Gregory. *The Future of Belief Debate*. New York: Herder and Herder, 1947.

Bourke, Vernon J. *St. Thomas and the Greek Moralists*. Milwaukee: Marquette University Press, 1947.

———. *The Essential Augustine*. New York: Mentor-Omega, 1964.

Bouyges, M., S.J. *Le Plan du Contra Gentiles de Saint Thomas*. Archives de Philosophie, 3 (1925), 176–197.

Brehier, Emile. *The History of Philosophy: The Hellenistic and Roman Age*. Tr. Wade Baskin. Chicago: University of Chicago Press, 1965.

Brennan, R. E., ed. *Essays in Thomism*. New York: Sheed and Ward, 1942.

———. *General Psychology: An Interpretation of the Science of Mind Based on Thomas Aquinas*. New York: Macmillan, 1937.

———. *The Image of His Maker* (Ch. 12). Milwaukee: Bruce Publishing Co., 1948.

———. *Thomist Psychology: A Philosophic Analysis of the Nature of Man*. New York: Macmillan, 1941.

Brisbois, E., S.J. "Desir Naturel et Vision de Dieu," *Nouvelle Revue Theologique*, 54 (1927), 81–97.

———. "The Natural and the Supernatural End of the Intellect," *New Scholasticism*, 5 (1931), 219–233.

Buckley, J. *Man's Last End*. St. Louis: Herder, 1949.

Callaghan, William J. *An Outline of the Philosophy of Aristotle*. Boston: Student Outline Co., 1959.

Caponigri, Robert A., ed. *Modern Catholic Thinkers*. New York: Harper Press, 1960.

Carriere, J. "Plotinus' Quest for Happiness," *Thomist,* 14 (Apr. 1951), 217–237.

Cathrein, V., S.J. "De Naturai Hominis Beatitudine," *Gregorianum,* II (1930), 398–409.

Cauchy, Venant. *Desir Naturel et Beatitude chez Saint Thomas.* Montreal: Fides, 1958.

Chesterton, G. K. *St. Thomas Aquinas.* New York: Sheed and Ward, 1933.

Compton, A.; J. Maritain; and others. *Man's Destiny in Eternity.* St. Louis: Herder, 1942.

Copleston, Frederick C., S.J. *Aquinas.* London: Penguin Books, 1955.

―――――. *A History of Philosophy.* New York: Image Books, 1950. Vol. II.

―――――. *Medieval Philosophy.* New York: Torch Books, 1961.

―――――. *St. Thomas and Nietzsche.* Oxford: Blackfriars, 1944.

Crehan, J. H. "Natural Happiness in Theology," *Month,* 184 (Dec. 1947), 278–286.

Cronin, M. *The Science of Ethics.* Dublin: Gill and Son, 1939. Vol. I.

Cunningham, R. L. "Hedonism," *New Catholic Encyclopedia,* 6:983–984. New York: McGraw-Hill, 1967.

Cusick, J. "Religious Life, Heaven as a Goal," *Catholic World,* 172 (Oct. 1950), 52–56.

Dalcourt, Gerald J. *The Philosophy of St. Thomas Aquinas.* New York: Monarch Press, 1965.

D'Arcy, Martin, S.J. *The Mind and Heart of Love.* New York: Meridan, 1956.

Deferrari, Roy J. *A Latin-English Dictionary of St. Thomas Aquinas.* Boston: St. Paul Press.

De la Vega, Francis Joseph, O.R.S.A. *Social Progress and Happiness in the Philosophy of St. Thomas Aquinas and Contemporary American Sociology.* Washington: Catholic University Press, 1949.

De Lubac, Henri, S.J. *Surnaturel.* Paris: Aubier, 1946.

Dewart, Leslie. *America.* New York: America Press, 1966.

Diggs, Bernard James. *Love and Being.* New York: S. F. Vanni, 1947.

Earle, William; James M. Edie; and John Wild. *Christianity and Existentialism.* Evanston: Northwestern University Press, 1963.

Elter, E., S.J. "De Naturali Hominis Beatitudine ad Mentem Scholae Antiquioris," *Gregorianum,* IX (1928), 269–306.

Farrell, Walter, O.P. *A Companion to the Summa;* Vol. II: *The Pursuit of Happiness.* New York: Sheed and Ward, 1939.

Freud, Sigmund. *Future of an Illusion.* Tr. W. D. Robson-Scott. London: Hogarth Press, 1949.

Gallagher, D. A. "Person, Beatitude and Society," *American Catholic Philosophical Association Proceedings* (1946), pp. 115–130.

Garrigou-Lagrange, Reginald, O.P. *God, His Existence and His Nature.* Tr. Dom. Bede Rose. St. Louis: Herder, 1934.

───────. *Reality: A Synthesis of Thomistic Thought.* Tr. Patrick Cummins, O.S.B. St. Louis: Herder, 1950. Vol. XIII.

Gilby, Thomas. *St. Thomas Aquinas :Theological Texts.* London: Oxford University Press, 1955.

───────. *St. Thomas Aquinas, Philosophical Texts.* London: Oxford University Press, 1951.

Gilson, Etienne. *The Christian Philosophy of St. Augustine.* Tr. L. E. M. Lynch. New York: Random House, 1960.

—————. *The Christian Philosophy of Thomas Aquinas.* New York: Random House, 1956.

—————. *God and Philosophy,* XIII. New Haven: Yale University Press, 1961.

—————. *The History of Christian Philosophy in the Middle Ages.* New York: Random House, 1955.

—————. *The Philosophy of St. Thomas Aquinas.* St. Louis: Herder, 1929.

—————. *The Spirit of Medieval Philoosphy.* Tr. A. H. C. Downes. New York: Scribner, 1936.

—————. *The Unity of Philosophical Experience.* New York: Scribner, 1937.

Gladstone, W. E., ed. *Works of Joseph Butler.* 2 vols. London: Oxford Press, 1897.

Gornall, Thomas. *A Philosophy of God.* New York: Sheed and Ward, 1963.

Grabman, Martin. *Introduction to the Theological Summa of St. Thomas.* St. Louis: Herder, 1930.

—————. *Thomas Aquinas.* New York: Longmans, 1928.

Grenier, Rev. Henri. *Thomistic Philosophy,* vol. 1. Tr. Rev. O'Hanley. Charlottetown, Canada: St. Dunstan's University Press, 1948.

Higgins, T. J. "The Deadlock among Non-Scholastics concerning the Definition of the Good," *Proceedings of the American Catholic Philosophical Association* (1958), p. 32.

Horman, Karl. *An Introduction to Moral Theology.* Westminster, Md.: Newman Press, 1963.

Joachim, H. H. *The Nichomachean Ethics, a Com-*

mentary. Ed. D. A. Rees. Oxford: Clarendon Press, 1951.

Kant, Immanuel. *Fundamental Principles of the Metaphysics of Morals*. Tr. Thomas K. Abbot. London: Longman, Green, 1923.

Kaufman, Walter. *The Faith of a Heretic*. Princeton, N. J.: Princeton University Press, 1961.

La Porta, A., O.S.B. "Les Notions d'Appetit Naturel et de Puissance Obedientelle chez Saint Thomas d'Aquin," *Ephemerides Theologicae Lovanienses*, 5 (1928), 257–277.

Lattey, C., ed. *St. Thomas Aquinas*. St. Louis: Herder, 1924.

Le Guillou, M. J. *Beatitude*. Chicago: Fides Publishing Co., 1956.

Lonergran, J. F. Bernard, S.J. "The Dehellenization of Dogma," *Theological Studies*, 28, no. 2 (June 1967), 336–351.

McDonough, A. "Enthusiasm for Heaven," *Sign*, 29 (Aug. 1949), 25.

McKeon, R. *Selections from Medieval Philosophies*. New York: Scribner, 1929.

————, ed. *The Basic Works of Aristotle*. New York: Random House, 1941.

Malevey, Leopold, S.J. "L'Esprit et le Desir de Dieu," *Nouvelle Revue Theologique*, 69 (1947), 3–31.

Maritain, Jacques. *The Degrees of Knowledge*. New York: Scribner, 1957.

————. *An Introduction to Philosophy*. New York: Sheed and Ward, 1934.

————. Ed. Ronald and Idella Gallagher. *A Maritain Reader*. New York: Sheed and Ward, 1934.

———. *Moral Philosophy*. New York: Scribner, 1964.

———. *Christianity and Philosophy*. New York: Scribner, 1964.

———. *The Peasant of the Garonne*. New York: Holt, Rinehart and Winston, 1968.

Maroux, Jean. *The Meaning of Man*. Garden City, N.Y.: Image, 1961.

Mauesberger, A. "Plato and Aristippus," *Hermes,* LXI (1926), 208–230.

Meyer, H. *The Philosophy of St. Thomas Aquinas*. Tr. Frederick Eckhoff. St. Louis: Herder, 1944.

Novak, Michael. "Belief and Mr. Dewart," *Commonweal,* Feb. 3, 1967 (pp. 485–488).

Nowicki, M. *Bibliography of Works in the Philosophy of History*. Mouton, 1964.

O'Connor, William R. *The Eternal Quest*. New York: Longmans, Green, 1947.

———. *The Natural Desire for God*. Milwaukee: Marquette University Press, 1948.

———. "The Natural Desire for God in St. Thomas," *New Scholasticism*, XIV, no. 3 (July 1940), 213–267.

———. "The Natural Desire for Happiness," *Modern Schoolman,* XXVI, no. 2 (Jan. 1949), 91–121.

———. "Some Historical Factors in the Development of the Concept of Human Finality," *Proceedings of the American Catholic Philosophical Association,* 23, (1949), 15–35.

O'Mahony, James E., O.S.F.C. *The Desire of God in the Philosophy of St. Thomas Aquinas*. Dublin: Cork University Press, 1929.

O'Neill, J. R. "Quest for Happiness," *Modern Schoolman*, 11 (Nov. 1933), 15–16.

Pegis, Anton C., ed. *Introduction to St. Thomas Aquinas*. New York: Random House, 1948.

———. "Matter, Beatitude and Liberty," *The Thomist*, 5 (1943), 265–280.

———. "Nature and Spirit: Some Reflections on the Problem of the End of Man," *Proceedings of the American Catholic Philosophical Association*, 23 (1949), 62–79.

Pfurtner, Stephanus. *Luther and Aquinas on Salvation*. Tr. Edward Quinn. New York: Sheed and Ward, 1964.

Pieper, Joseph. *The Human Wisdom of St. Thomas*. New York: Sheed and Ward, 1948.

———. *Guide to Thomas Aquinas*. Tr. Richard and Clara Winston. New York: Mentor Press, 1962.

———. *Introduction to Thomas Aquinas*. Tr. Richard and Clara Winston. London: Faber and Faber, 1962.

———. *Happiness and Contemplation*. Chicago: Henry Regnery Co., 1958.

Plantinga, Alvin, ed. *Faith and Philosophy: Philosophical Studies in Religion and Ethics*. Grand Rapids, Mich.: Eerdmans, 1964.

Prestige, G. *God in Patristic Thought*. London: P. Allen, 1936.

Prime, J. F. T. "Mystery of Human Motive," *Blackfriars*, 29 (May 1948), 237–239.

Ramirez, J. M., O.P. "De Hominis Beatitudine," *Matriti: Consejo Superior de Investigaciones Cientificas* (1943).

Reutemann, Brother Charles, F.S.C. *The Thomistic*

Concept of Pleasures as Compared with Hedonistic and Rigoristic Philosophies. Washington: Catholic University Press, 1953.

Rickaby, Josh, S.J. *The Moral Teaching of St. Thomas.* London: Burns and Oates, 1896.

—————. *Of God and His Creatures.* Westminster, Md: Canell Press, 1950.

Roland-Gosselin, O.P. "Le Desir du Bonheur et L'Existence de Dieu," *Revue des Sciences Philosophiques et Theologiques,* vol. 13 (1924).

—————. "Beatitude et Desir Naturel d'apres S. Thomas d'Aquin," *Revue des Sciences Philosophigiques,* 18 (1929) 193–222.

Ross, W. D., and others, eds. *The Works of Aristotle.* 11 vols. Oxford: Clarendon Press, 1928–1931.

Rousselot, Pierre, S.J. *The Intellectualism of Saint Thomas.* Tr. James E. O'Mahony O.F.M.Cap. New York: Sheed and Ward, 1935.

Rueve, Stephen, S.J. "Aristotle on Happiness and Pleasures," *Modern Schoolman,* 13 (May 1936), 82–84.

Sarvey, W. "A Defense of Hedonism Ethics," *An International Journal of Social, Political and Legal Philosophy,* 45 (Oct. 1934), 1–26.

Schapp, Ludwig, and others. *Fathers of the Church.* 16 vols. New York: CIMA Publishing Co., 1948.

Schwinn, Bonaventure. "Review of the Eternal Quest," *Commonweal,* 47 (Feb. 13, 1948), p. 452.

Sheed, F. J. *Theology and Sanity.* New York: Sheed and Ward, 1946.

Sheedy, C. E. *The Christian Virtues.* South Bend, Ind.: University of Notre Dame Press, 1949.

Sheehan, Robert J. *The Philosophy of Happiness*

According to St. Thomas Aquinas (an abstract). Washington: Catholic University Press, 1956.

Sheldon, W. H. "The Absolute Truth of Hedonism," *Journal of Philosophy,* 48 (May 11, 1950), 285–304.

Smith, Elwood F., and Louis A. Ryan. *Preface to Happiness.* New York: Benziger, 1950.

Smith, G., S.J. "The Natural End of Man," *Proceedings of the American Catholic Philosophical Association,* 23 (1949), 47–61.

Smith, G. D. *The Teaching of the Catholic Church.* New York: Macmillan, 1948 (vol. I).

Smith, Ignatius, O.P. *Classification of Desires in St. Thomas and in Modern Sociology.* Washington: Catholic University Press, 1915.

Vann, Gerald. *St. Thomas Aquinas.* New York: Benziger, 1947.

Verhaar, John W. M., S.J. "Dewart and the New Neo Thomism," *Continuum,* vol. 5, no. 4 (1968).

Vogt, Bernard O.F.M. "The Metaphysics of Human Liberty in Duns Scotus," *Proceedings of the American Catholic Philosophical Association,* 16 (1940), 27–37.

Walz, A., O.P. *St. Thomas Aquinas, a Biographical Study.* Tr. S. Bullough. Westminster, Md.: Canęll Press, 1951.

Watson, John. *Hedonistic Theories from Aristippus to Spencer.* Glasgow: John MacLehase and Sons, 1895.

Wilhelmsen, Frederick. "Leslie Dewart: Heretic or Helene," *Triumph* (Jan. 1967).

Wilms, Jerome. *Divine Friendship.* Dubuque: Priory Press, 1958.

Wordman, A. E., and J. L. Creed. *The Philosophy of Aristotle*. New York: Mentor Books, 1963.

Wright, William Kelley. *The Ethical Significance of Feeling, Pleasure and Happiness in Modern Non-Hedonistic Systems*. Chicago: University of Chicago Press, 1907.

EXISTENTIALISM AND ITS IMPLICATIONS FOR COUNSELING ...... .75
M. Emmanuel Fontes

A study in depth which leads to seven general principles for integrating existential insights into counseling.

THE CREATION OF FULL HUMAN PERSONALITY ...... .75
Joseph Drew & William Hague

Complete psychological growth is a process inseparable from total reality—biological and spiritual, internal and external. Vocation is important.

NEW EDUCATIONAL METHODS FOR INCREASING RELIGIOUS EFFECTIVENESS ... .75
Dean C. Dauw

Special group methods of self-education that have proved helpful to others are also helpful to religious organizations.

LOVE AND SELFISHNESS ...... .75
Alice von Hildebrand

True love cannot be separated from a joyful readiness to make enduring sacrifices for the sake of the beloved.

A PSYCHOLOGY OF THE CATHOLIC INTELLECTUAL ...... .75
Adrian van Kaam

The split between secular and religious learning rooted in psychological history must be healed to prevent disaster.

EMOTIONAL DEVELOPMENT AND SPIRITUAL GROWTH ...... .75
Timothy J. Gannon

To what extent can insights into a man's emotional life contribute to the solution of problems of spiritual growth.

WHAT'S WRONG WITH GOD .75
Thomas M. Steeman

A probing search into a question that has practical ramifications for the modern man.

HELPING THE DISTURBED RELIGIOUS .75
E.F. Doherty

Like everybody else religious have problems of tensions and anxieties. Their causes and manner of handling are treated with sensitive insight.

WORLD POVERTY ... CAN IT BE SOLVED? .75
Barbara Ward

In depth analysis of the problem of world poverty with sensible suggestions on how to solve it.

THE PRIESTHOOD: MASCULINE AND CELIBATE .75
Conrad W. Baars, M.D.

Psychiatrist, author, and consultant on the problems of the priesthood at the 1971 Vatican Synod of Bishops, Dr. Baars develops the positive values of celibacy and a regimen to achieve a priesthood both celibate and masculine.

THE RIDDLE OF GENESIS .75
Robert Koch

The study of comparative religion and modern biblical exegesis help to convey the essential message of the first eleven chapters of Genesis.

THE CHURCH TODAY .75

Important studies by men like Ratzinger, Schweizer, Congar, Pauwels and Winkhofer on various aspects of the Church in the modern world.

HOW TO TREAT AND PREVENT THE CRISIS IN THE PRIESTHOOD .... .75
Conrad Baars, M.D.

A well-known psychiatrist, from vast experiences, discusses the role of the Church in the causation, treatment and prevention of the crisis in the priesthood.

THE MESSAGE OF CHRIST AND THE COUNSELOR $1.50
John Quesnel

An expert discusses the principles of counseling in general and pastoral counseling in particular as gleaned from the life of Christ.

TEMPTATIONS FOR THE THEOLOGY OF LIBERATION .... .75
Bonaventure Kloppenburg O.F.M.

A member of the Papal Theological Commission warns against the various temptations to water down, distort or belittle theology and the Gospel message. A clear voice in babel of confusion.

THE FAMILY PLANNING DILEMMA REVISITED $1.25
John G. Quesnell

Since the publication of **Humane Vitae** a lot of study has been given to family planning. This booklet looks at the new insights in the light of the teaching of the Church. His is an optimistic approach.

RENEWAL AND RECONCILIATION .... .75
Reflections for a Holy Year
Msgr. James O'Reilly

The world, the Church, the family and society plus the sacramental system are discussed within the context of renewal and reconciliation. These reflections are appropriate for any year.

POLITICAL STRUGGLE OF ACTIVE HOMOSEXUALS TO GAIN SOCIAL ACCEPTANCE $1.50
George Kelly

Having learned from civil rights movements, overt homosexuals are exerting strong and expert political pressure to affect public mores.

TO WHOM SHALL WE GO? .... .75
Zachary Hayes O.F.M.

Christ and the mystery of man is the theme of this booklet. It fills a gap as it focuses on the place of Christology in the Church today.

THE MORAL PROBLEMS OF CONTRACEPTION .... .75
Msgr. James O'Reilly

This booklet discusses the objective morality, without imputing subjective blame, of the contraceptive act. Contraception is regarded as a devaluation of a basic human good, namely the power to initiate human life.

THE SPIRITUAL DIRECTOR $2.00
Damien Isabell O.F.M.

This is a practical guide for spiritual direction on which growth depends. It contains and overview of approaches and an invaluable bibliography.

THE SACRAMENT OF PENANCE AND RECONCILIATION .... .75
Msgr. George A. Kelly

This is a sociological and historical study of the changes of attitude and practice of the Sacrament of Reconciliation.

THE HOMOSEXUALS SEARCH FOR HAPPINESS $1.25
Conrad W. Baars, M.D.

In this psycho-philosophical approach Dr. Baars treats homosexuality with remarkable compassion and understanding. He points out that the pressing need is personal, individual affirmation.

THE NATURE AND MEANING OF
CHASTITY $1.25
William E. May, Ph.D.

Chastity is a loving integration of sex and affection into our lives enabling us, as sexual beings, to love and be loved. This definition is explained in detail.

LAY AND RELIGIOUS STATES OF
LIFE: THEIR DISTINCTION AND
COMPLEMENTARITY .... .75
James O'Reilly

The distinction between the lay and religious states of life must be maintained because of the nature of the movement of man toward salvation and the effect of the environment of life in the world.

THE PASCHAL MYSTERY:
CORE GRACE IN THE LIFE OF THE
CHRISTIAN .... .75
Augustine Paul Hennesy C.P.

Christian hope lies in the Risen Christ. Christians must learn to take on Christ's attitude toward the cross and the glory of it.

VALUING SUFFERING AS A
CHRISTIAN: SOME PSYCHOLOGICAL
PERSPECTIVES .... .75
Henry C. Simmons C.P.

Within the mystery of the cross of Christ, the sufferings of daily life hold meaning and value. Christian hope lies in the promises of Christ's death and resurrection.

SEX, LOVE AND PROCREATION .... .75
William E. May

This booklet is concerned with the important question: Can sexual intercourse as an act of love ever be separated from intercourse as a creative act?

AN UNCERTAIN CHURCH THE NEW CATHOLIC PROBLEM 75
George A. Kelly and John A. Flynn

In a clear, concise manner this booklet explores the foundations of academic freedom. It is also a reaffirmation of the great Catholic heritage in intellectual circles.

ROOTS OF HUMAN RIGHTS $2.25
Edward W. O'Rourke, Bishop of Peoria

The most significant events of the past two decades have involved the struggle of individuals and nations for human rights. If the 1980's are to bring a resolution of these struggles, there must be a deeper understanding of human rights.

THE NEED FOR THE MAGISTERIUM OF THE CHURCH .... .75
K.D. Whitehead

God has established the sacred magisterium in his Church. In a matter as fundamental as our eternal salvation, there has to be a court of appeal to which we have recourse for decisions in answer to the many questions which arise in every age, in every life.

THE UNITY OF THE MORAL AND THE SPIRITUAL LIFE .... .75
William E. May

The uneasiness many have experienced in integrating their lives as members of a worshipping community with their daily concern and their obligations as parents and citizens is not unresolvable. The moral and spiritual lives are compatible.

THE DIFFERENCE THAT JESUS MAKES: THE SACRAMENT OF THE FORGIVING GOD $1.25
Robert Kress

The New Covenant, in the blood of Jesus, is not new in the sense that it existed before. It is new in that it brings to perfection what God has been planning and doing all along—loving, gracing, and living in communion with human beings.

CONTEMPORARY CULTURE AND CHRISTIANITY $1.50
Maurice DeLange

A man-centered society is usually tempted to say that the ultimate meaning in life is absurdity and nothingness. A god-centered society, wherein love is shared with fellow men and women, can indeed show the real meaning of life.

THE QUEST FOR SECURITY $3.50
Alfred Martin O.F.M.

Every age has its own panacea. In our time it is a quest for security. We all want security of all kinds—economic, social, material, mental. But security is a state of mind with religion as an essential element.

MENTAL HEALTH: PSYCHOTHERAPY OF TOMORROW $2.50
Alfred Martin O.F.M.

Because there is an intimate relationship between body and soul, what affects one will affect the other. This mutual influence has a pervading effect on mental health.

MINISTRY TO THE SICK AND DYING:
The Pastoral Reflection Paper............... $1.75
(Washington Theological Union)
Jude J. McGeehan O.F.M.

Christ is the Divine Physician of mankind . . . Because sickness cannot be separated from its religious import in the history of salvation, the Apostolate to the Sick is one of the most essential missions of the Church.

MINIMUM ORDER $5.00

Synthesis Series is published by
FRANCISCAN HERALD PRESS
1434 WEST 51st STREET
CHICAGO, ILLINOIS 60609